Cooking with
Irish Whiskey

Contents

Introduction

There are those who maintain that the Irish discovered the art of distilling and others who even go so far as to say it was a gift from St Patrick himself.

Lighter, with higher alcohol content, Irish Whiskey is matured for five to fifteen years before reaching the market under labels such as Tullamore Dew, Jameson's, Bushmill's, Coleraine, Paddy's, Hewitt's, Murphy's, Power's, Dunphy's and Midleton.

Whiskey is best drunk with just a little water to release the flavours. But good cooks can never resist a fine ingredient, and so they have created wonderful recipes such as those collected here. Whiskey is flambéed with shellfish and meat, poured into Christmas cakes to give more cheer to the season and added to coffee to create that masterpiece which is Irish Coffee.

All these recipes are best made with true Irish Whiskey, but if you prefer to keep your Irish for drinking, they can also be made with Scotch, or American Bourbon, Rye, Corn or Sour Mash.

Whiskey Terrine

125 G/4 OZ BUTTER

1 LARGE ONION, CHOPPED

1 CLOVE GARLIC, CRUSHED

125 G/4 OZ STREAKY BACON, RINDED AND CHOPPED

250 G/8 OZ CHICKEN LIVERS

125 G/4 OZ BUTTON MUSHROOMS

150 ML/¼ PINT WHISKEY

FINELY GRATED RIND OF 1 LEMON

2 TABLESPOONS LEMON JUICE

1½ TABLESPOONS CHOPPED FRESH PARSLEY

2½ TABLESPOONS FRESH WHITE BREADCRUMBS

2 SMALL BAY LEAVES

3 ALLSPICE BERRIES

SALT AND FRESHLY GROUND BLACK PEPPER

1 Melt the butter in a large pan. Add the onion and garlic and cook gently for 10 minutes. Add the bacon, chicken livers and mushrooms and cook for 5 minutes. Add the whiskey, lemon rind, lemon juice and season to taste. Cover and simmer gently for 10-15 minutes.

2 Purée in a food processor or blender until smooth. Add the parsley and breadcrumbs and blend again to mix.

3 Spoon into a serving dish and level the surface. Press the bay leaves and berries into the top. Cover and chill to set.

Serves 6

Whiskey Steaks Dijonnaise

6 FILLET STEAKS

1 CLOVE GARLIC, CRUSHED

50 G/2 OZ BUTTER

2 TABLESPOONS VEGETABLE OIL

250 G/8 OZ BUTTON MUSHROOMS, SLICED

5 TABLESPOONS WHISKEY

2 TABLESPOONS HERB MUSTARD

200 ML/7 FL OZ BEEF STOCK

SALT AND FRESHLY GROUND BLACK PEPPER

WATERCRESS SPRIGS, TO GARNISH

1 Season the steaks on both sides with salt, pepper and garlic.

2 Heat the butter and oil in a large frying pan. Add the steaks and fry over a moderate heat for 2–3 minutes on each side to seal and brown. Cook for a further 1–3 minutes on each side, until the steaks are done to your liking. Remove from the pan and keep warm.

3 Add the mushrooms to the pan, fry for 1–2 minutes, then add the whiskey, mustard and stock. Bring to the boil, stirring continuously, and season to taste.

4 Return the steaks to the pan and turn to coat throughly in the sauce. Transfer to a warmed serving dish, pour over the sauce and garnish with watercress sprigs.

5 Serve at once with sauté potatoes, carrots and mangetout.

Serves 6

Whiskey Beef Pot Roast

6 STRIPS PORK FAT

150 ML/¼ PINT WHISKEY

1 X 1.25 G/2½ LB BONED BEEF TOPSIDE

3 CARROTS, SLICED

1 BOUQUET GARNI

450 ML/¾ PINT RED WINE

¼ TEASPOON GRATED NUTMEG

50 G/2 OZ BEEF DRIPPING

15 G/½ OZ BUTTER

1 TABLESPOON PLAIN FLOUR

SALT AND FRESHLY GROUND BLACK PEPPER

1 Soak the pork fat in the whiskey for 1 hour. Drain, reserving the whiskey. Insert the strips into the beef using a larding needle. Place in a bowl with carrots, bouquet garni, whiskey, wine, nutmeg and seasoning to taste. Cover and leave to marinate overnight.

2 Drain the beef, reserving the marinade. Melt the dripping in a casserole dish. Put in the beef and brown. Pour in the marinade and bring to the boil. Cover and simmer for 2 hours or until tender. Transfer to a serving dish.

3 Skim off any fat from the cooking liquid, strain and return to pan. Mix the butter with flour forming a paste. Add a little of the liquid, mix well, then stir into the pan. Simmer, stirring until thickened. Serve the beef with the sauce.

Serves 6-8

Steaks with Green Peppercorn Sauce

25 G/1 OZ BUTTER

2 TABLESPOONS SUNFLOWER OIL

4 FILLET STEAKS, ABOUT 1 CM/½ INCH THICK

2 TABLESPOONS WHISKEY

150 ML/¼ PINT DOUBLE CREAM

1 CLOVE GARLIC, CRUSHED

2 TEASPOONS GREEN PEPPERCORNS

1 TABLESPOON CHOPPED PARSLEY

A PINCH OF SALT

PARSLEY SPRIGS, TO GARNISH

1 Melt the butter in the oil in a large frying pan. Add the steaks and fry for about 2 minutes on each side. Warm the whiskey, pour over the steaks and ignite with a lighted taper. Once the flames have died down remove the steaks from the pan and keep warm.

2 Add the cream, garlic, peppercorns, parsley and salt to the fat remaining in the pan. Cook, stirring continuously, for 1 minute on a low heat, until heated through. Return the steaks to the pan and cook for 2 minutes on each side, or according to taste.

3 Garnish with parsley sprigs and serve with new potatoes, carrots and courgettes.

Serves 4

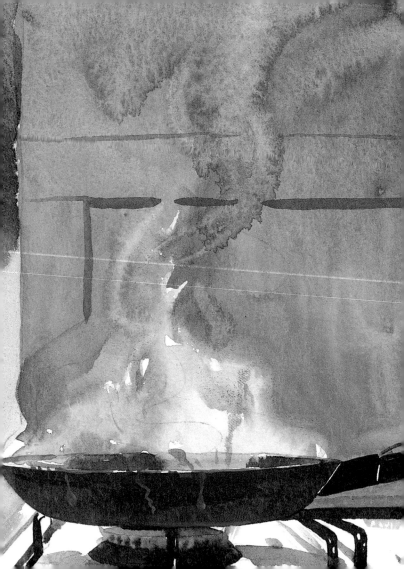

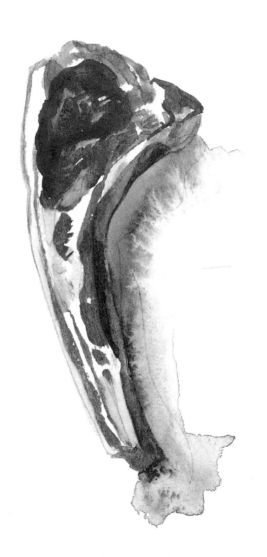

Whiskey Lamb Chops

4 LAMB CHOPS

6 TABLESPOONS WHISKEY

25 G/1 OZ BUTTER

1 TABLESPOON FRESHLY CHOPPED MINT

2 ONIONS, FINELY GRATED

75 G/3 OZ CHEDDAR CHEESE, GRATED

FOR THE SAUCE:

40 G/1½ OZ BUTTER

40 G/1½ OZ FLOUR

150 ML/¼ PINT MILK

2 CLOVES GARLIC, CRUSHED

SALT AND FRESHLY GROUND BLACK PEPPER

1 Place the chops in a dish and pour over the whiskey. Cover and leave to marinate overnight. Drain reserving the liquid. Brown the chops in a pan in the butter. Place in an ovenproof dish and sprinkle with mint and onions.

2 Melt the butter for the sauce in a pan and stir in flour. Cook for 2 minutes then gradually stir in milk. Bring to the boil, adding garlic and seasoning. Simmer for 5 minutes. Remove from heat and stir in whiskey liquid. Pour over chops and top with cheese.

3 Cook in a preheated oven, 190°C (375°F) Gas Mark 5 for 30-40 minutes.

Serves 4

Gaelic Pork

25 G/1 OZ BUTTER

1 TABLESPOON SUNFLOWER OIL

1 CLOVE GARLIC, FINELY SLICED

4 PORK ESCALOPES

130 ML/4½ FL OZ IRISH WHISKEY

25 G/1 OZ FLOUR

300 ML/½ PINT DRY WHITE WINE

150 ML/¼ PINT CRÈME FRAÎCHE

SALT AND FRESHLY GROUND BLACK PEPPER

1 TABLESPOON CHOPPED FRESH CHIVES, TO GARNISH

1 Gently heat the butter and oil in a frying pan, and sauté the garlic for a few minutes until golden. Remove the garlic and reserve. Increase the heat, add the escalopes and seal on each side. Reduce the heat and cook gently for 10 minutes or until cooked through, turning once half way.

2 Warm the whiskey in a ladle, pour over escalopes and ignite. When the flames die down remove the escalopes and keep hot. Sprinkle the flour into the juices, stir well and cook for 1 minute. Stir in the wine and simmer for 2 minutes, stirring. Add the crème fraîche and season to taste. Reheat almost to boiling point and add the garlic.

3 Place the pork escalopes on warmed plates and pour the sauce over. Garnish with chives and serve.

Serves 4

Pork in Pastry

500 G/1 LB PORK FILLET

2 TABLESPOONS WHISKEY

1 TABLESPOON MUSTARD

25 G/1 OZ BUTTER

1 TABLESPOON OIL

2 TEASPOONS CHOPPED FRESH MIXED HERBS

250 G/8 OZ FROZEN PUFF PASTRY, THAWED

1 EGG, BEATEN

SALT AND FRESHLY GROUND BLACK PEPPER

1 Cut the pork into 4 portions and trim the edges. Mix the whiskey, mustard and seasoning to taste in a dish.

2 Marinate the pork in this mixture for several hours in the refrigerator, turning often. Remove and pat dry.

3 Heat the butter and oil in a frying pan and quickly fry the fillets until golden on both sides. Cool completely and sprinkle with herbs. Roll out the pastry thinly and cut into 4 portions. Wrap each fillet neatly in pastry, sealing the joins with the egg. Use the trimmings to make decorative shapes and attach to the dough with egg.

4 Chill for at least 1 hour, then glaze the tops with the remaining egg and bake in a preheated oven 190°C (375°F) Gas Mark 5 for 20 minutes. Reduce the heat to 160°C (325°F) Gas Mark 3 and bake for a further 15 minutes.

Serves 4

Chicken with Irish Whiskey

45 G/1¾ OZ BUTTER

125 G/4 OZ STREAKY BACON, RINDED AND DICED

2 LARGE ONIONS, SLICED

1 x 1.5 KG/3 LB ROASTING CHICKEN, JOINTED

2 TABLESPOONS WHISKEY

1 75 CL BOTTLE RED WINE

2 GARLIC CLOVES, CRUSHED

1 BOUQUET GARNI

250 G/8 OZ SMALL BUTTON MUSHROOMS

20 G/¾ OZ PLAIN FLOUR

SALT AND FRESHLY GROUND BLACK PEPPER

1 Melt 25 g/1 oz of butter in a casserole dish, add bacon and onions and cook until onions soften. Set aside. Add chicken and brown all over. Warm the whiskey, pour over chicken and ignite.
When flames subside, return bacon and onions to casserole.
2 Heat the wine in a pan and pour over chicken. Season to taste. Add garlic and bouquet garni. Cover and cook in a preheated oven at 180°C (350°F) Gas Mark 4 for 1 hour.
3 Add mushrooms and cook for 15 minutes more. Remove bouquet garni. Return the casserole to the stove, mix flour and remaining butter to a paste. Add to the casserole and bring just to the boil, stirring until the sauce has thickened.
Serves 4

Pheasant with Whiskey

A delicious and unusual dinner party dish.

40 G/1½ OZ BUTTER
1-2 PHEASANTS, DEPENDING ON SIZE, CLEANED AND TRUSSED
1 ONION, FINELY CHOPPED
85-120 ML/3-4 FL OZ WHISKEY
150 ML/¼ PINT BEEF STOCK
A PINCH OF CAYENNE PEPPER
4-6 JUNIPER BERRIES
120 ML/4 FL OZ DOUBLE OR WHIPPING CREAM
½ TEASPOON LEMON JUICE
SALT AND FRESHLY GROUND BLACK PEPPER
WATERCRESS, TO GARNISH

1 Melt the butter in a casserole dish and brown the pheasant on all sides. Remove with a slotted spoon. Add the onion and cook until soft.

2 Warm half the whiskey in a ladle. Return pheasant to the pan, pour whiskey over and ignite. Add stock, cayenne, seasoning and juniper berries. Bring to the boil. Cook in a preheated oven at 190°C (375°F) Gas Mark 5 for 1 hour or until tender. When tender, remove from pan and joint it.

3 Boil the sauce until syrupy, add remaining whiskey, cream and lemon juice. Reheat without boiling.

4 Strain the sauce over the meat and garnish with watercress.

Serves 3-4

Veal with Irish Whiskey

90 G/3½ OZ BUTTER

750 G/1¾ LB LEG OF VEAL, BONED AND CUBED

2 SMALL ONIONS

1 BOUQUET GARNI

300 ML/½ PINT WHITE WINE

300 ML/½ PINT CHICKEN STOCK

40 G/1½ OZ FLOUR

4 TABLESPOONS DOUBLE CREAM

2 TABLESPOONS WHISKEY

SALT AND FRESHLY GROUND BLACK PEPPER

PARSLEY SPRIGS, TO GARNISH

1 Melt 50 g/2 oz of the butter in a pan and fry the veal until well sealed. Transfer to a casserole. Add the onions and bouquet garni.

2 Bring the wine to the boil, season and pour over veal. Cover and cook in a preheated oven at 160°C (325°F) Gas Mark 3 for 1 hour or until tender. Discard onions and bouquet garni. Strain off the liquid and boil rapidly in a pan until reduced to 450 ml/¾ pint. Keep the veal warm.

3 Cream the remaining butter with flour; gradually whisk into the sauce until thickened. Simmer for 3 minutes, adjust seasoning and add the cream.

4 Warm the whiskey, pour over the veal and ignite. Pour the sauce over the veal and garnish with parsley sprigs.

Serves 4

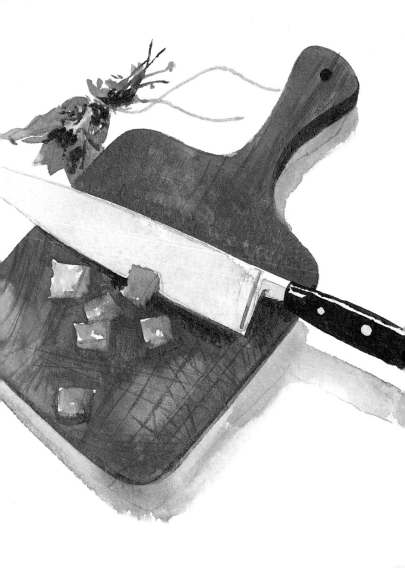

Crab Bisque with Whiskey

1 CRAB, WEIGHING ABOUT 500 G/1 LB

1 ONION, CHOPPED

2 CARROTS, CHOPPED

2 CELERY STICKS, SLICED

1 BOUQUET GARNI

40 G/1½ OZ BUTTER

40 G/1½ OZ PLAIN FLOUR

1 TABLESPOON LEMON JUICE

150 ML/¼ PINT WHITE WINE

25 G/1 OZ LONG GRAIN RICE

4 TABLESPOONS DOUBLE CREAM

2-3 TABLESPOONS WHISKEY

SALT AND FRESHLY GROUND BLACK PEPPER

1 Remove both the brown and white crab meat from the cleaned shell and chop. Chill. Break up the shell and put it into a pan with the onion, carrots, celery, bouquet garni and 1.5 litres/2½ pints of water. Boil, then cover and simmer for 45 minutes. Strain the liquid and reserve.

2 Melt the butter in a pan, stir in the flour and cook for about 1-2 minutes. Gradually add the crab stock and boil. Add the lemon juice, wine and rice and simmer for 10 minutes, stirring occasionally.

3 Add the crab and simmer for 10 minutes more. Add the cream and seasoning. Reheat, stirring in the whiskey.

Serves 4

Kipper Pâté

A delicious way to start a meal.

350 G/12 OZ KIPPER FILLETS
75 G/3 OZ BUTTER, MELTED
3 TABLESPOONS WHISKEY
FRESHLY GROUND BLACK PEPPER
4 SMALL GHERKINS OR TOMATO SLICES, TO GARNISH

1 Place the fillets in a large frying pan of gently simmering water and poach for 10 minutes. Remove from the pan with a fish slice and drain on kitchen paper. Alternatively, put a piece of foil on to the wire tray of a grill pan and place the fillets on top and grill for 5 minutes on each side.

2 Allow to cool slightly then remove the skin and any stray bones.

3 Place the kippers in a food processor or blender. Add the melted butter and process until smooth. Add the whiskey and pepper and process again.

4 Spoon into 4 small pots and refrigerate, overnight if possible. The flavour of this improves if made the day before. Serve garnished with gherkins or tomato slices.

Serves 4

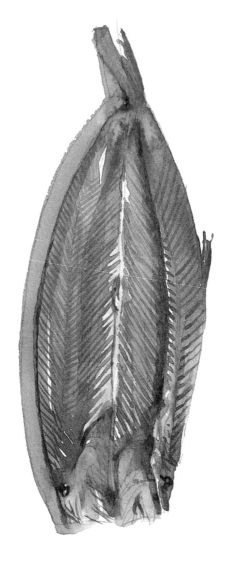

Whiskey Prawns

4 TABLESPOONS OIL

60 G/2 OZ BUTTER

2 SHALLOTS, FINELY CHOPPED

1 CLOVE GARLIC, CRUSHED

500 G/1 LB GREEN PRAWNS, SHELLED AND DEVEINED

2 RIPE TOMATOES, PEELED, DESEEDED AND DICED

A TINY PINCH OF CAYENNE PEPPER

130 ML/4½ FL OZ WHISKEY

130 ML/4½ FL OZ DRY WHITE WINE

75 ML/3 FL OZ CREAM

1 TABLESPOON CORNFLOUR MIXED WITH 1 TABLESPOON MILK

1 EGG YOLK

SALT AND FRESHLY GROUND BLACK PEPPER

1 Heat the oil in a frying pan, melt the butter, add shallots
and garlic and cook for 3 minutes.

2 Add prawns, tomatoes, salt, pepper and cayenne pepper and
cook until prawns change colour.

3 Pour over half the whiskey, ignite and shake pan until flames subside.
Add wine and simmer for 3 minutes. Remove prawns and keep warm.
Add remaining whiskey and cream to pan and boil, add cornflour
mixture, stirring until it boils again. Stir a little sauce into the
egg yolk, return to pan and stir for 1 minute without boiling.
Pour over the prawns and serve immediately.

Serves 4-6

Scallops Flamed in Irish Whiskey

Whiskey gives a perfect edge to this sumptuous dish.

12 SCALLOPS IN THEIR SHELLS
125 G/4 OZ BUTTER
6 SHALLOTS OR 1 LARGE MILD ONION, FINELY SLICED
2 CLOVES GARLIC, CRUSHED
150 ML/¼ PINT WHISKEY
250 ML/8 FL OZ FISH OR VEGETABLE STOCK
SALT AND FRESHLY GROUND BLACK PEPPER
SPRIGS OF CHERVIL, TO GARNISH

1 Detach the scallops from their shells and scrape off the beard-like fringe and intestinal thread, keep the orange coral attached to the white section. Scrub and reserve the shells.

2 Melt the butter in a pan, and fry the shallots or onion until golden. Add the garlic and scallops and cook for 1 minute on each side or until the white sections become opaque.

3 Warm the whiskey in a pan, pour over the scallops. Light the whiskey and when the flames have subsided, remove the scallops and keep warm. Add the stock to the pan, bring to a boil, reduce to 125 ml/4 fl oz and season to taste.

4 Place 3 scrubbed scallop shells on each plate and arrange a scallop on each shell. Spoon over the whiskey mixture, scatter with sprigs of chervil and serve immediately.

Serves 4

Irish Lobster

This is a traditional Irish dish using uncooked lobster but it can also be made with lightly cooked lobster.

1 VERY FRESH LOBSTER, CHOPPED
50 G/2 OZ BUTTER
3 SHALLOTS, FINELY CHOPPED
50 ML/2 FL OZ WHISKEY, WARMED
150 ML/¼ PINT CREAM OR CRÉME FRAÎCHE
SALT AND FRESHLY GROUND BLACK PEPPER
CHOPPED FRESH PARSLEY, TO GARNISH

1 Open up the lobster back-side down and, with a sharp knife, cut in half lengthways, taking care not to damage the shell. Extract the meat from the tail, body, head and claws. Reserve the shells.
2 Heat 25 g/1 oz of the butter in a pan and add the lobster, season to taste. Gently sauté for a few minutes until the meat becomes opaque and set aside.
3 Melt the remaining butter and gently fry the shallots until transparent. Return the lobster to the heat and pour over the whiskey and ignite, when the flames have subsided add the cream or créme fraîche and cook gently for a few minutes.
4 Pour into the lobster shells and garnish with parsley and serve hot with fresh crusty bread.

Serves 2

Chocolate Marquise

Rich, sweet and with a slight hint of oranges this tempting dessert is a must for all chocolate lovers!

165 G/5½ OZ PLAIN CHOCOLATE
2 TABLESPOONS WHISKEY
90 G/3½ OZ UNSALTED BUTTER, SOFTENED
50 G/2 OZ ICING SUGAR
2 EGGS, SEPARATED
20 G/¾ OZ CASTER SUGAR
1 ORANGE, SEGMENTED, TO SERVE

1 Break the chocolate into pieces and place in a heatproof bowl with 1 tablespoon of water and the whiskey. Stand over a pan of simmering water until the chocolate melts. Remove the bowl from the pan. Stir the chocolate well and allow 5 minutes to cool.

2 Cream the softened butter and icing sugar. Beat in the egg yolks, then fold in the melted chocolate.

3 Whisk the egg whites and caster sugar until very stiff and fold into the chocolate mixture. Pour into a 600 ml/1 pint mould or 4 individual moulds lined with foil, and chill until set.

4 To serve, dip the mould in hot water for a few seconds to loosen the marquise from the sides, turn out on to a dish. Peel off the foil and serve with orange segments.

Serves 4

Hazelnut and Whiskey Whip

A light and nutty dessert with a hint of whiskey to complement any meal.

50 G/2 OZ HAZELNUTS, SKINNED AND FINELY CHOPPED
50 G/2 OZ DEMERARA SUGAR
50 G/2 OZ WHOLEMEAL BREADCRUMBS
275 ML/9 FL OZ DOUBLE CREAM
150 G/5 OZ NATURAL YOGURT
3 TABLESPOONS WHISKEY
1 TABLESPOON CLEAR HONEY

1 Combine the hazelnuts, sugar and breadcrumbs and place on a baking sheet. Put under a preheated hot grill until golden brown, stirring frequently. Leave to cool.

2 Whip the cream until it stands in soft peaks then whip in the yogurt, whiskey and honey. Fold in the hazelnut mixture, spoon into individual dishes and chill before serving.

Serves 6–8

Chocolate and Whiskey Pots

Chocolate and whiskey go well together and this dessert is perfect for any special occasion.

175 G/6 OZ PLAIN CHOCOLATE
25 G/1 OZ UNSALTED BUTTER
3 EGGS, SEPARATED
2 TABLESPOONS WHISKEY
1 EGG WHITE
LANGUE DE CHAT BISCUITS, TO SERVE

1 Break the chocolate into small pieces and place in a heatproof bowl with the butter. Stand the bowl over a pan of simmering water until the chocolate has melted.
2 Beat the egg yolks and whiskey into the chocolate and chill until cool, but do not allow the mixture to set. Whisk all 4 egg whites until stiff and fold into the chocolate mixture.
3 Pour into 4 x 150 ml/¼ pint ramekin dishes or 6 x 100 ml/ 4 fl oz chocolate pots. Chill for at least 6 hours until set.
4 Serve with langue de chat biscuits.

Serves 4-6

Irish Whiskey Cake

RIND OF 1 LEMON
75 ML/3 FL OZ IRISH WHISKEY
175 G/6 OZ BUTTER
175 G/6 OZ CASTER SUGAR
3 EGGS, SEPARATED
175 G/6 OZ PLAIN FLOUR, SIFTED
175 G/6 OZ SULTANAS
A PINCH OF SALT
1 TEASPOON BAKING POWDER

1 Put the lemon rind into a glass, cover with the whiskey and leave overnight, covered.

2 Cream the butter and sugar until light. Add the egg yolks one at a time with a spoonful of sifted flour, mixing well. Strain the whiskey into it and add the sultanas with 2 tablespoons of flour.

3 Whisk the egg whites until stiff and fold into the mixture with the remaining flour mixed with the salt and baking powder. See that the mixture is well mixed together.

4 Pour into a greased and lined 17.5 cm/7 inch cake tin and bake in a preheated oven at 180°C (350°F) Gas Mark 4 for 1½–1¾ hours. Test with a skewer before taking from the oven - the skewer should come out clean.

5 Cool for 5 minutes in the tin, then turn out on to a wire rack and remove the paper.

Makes a 17.5 cm/7 inch cake

Whiskey Fruit Cake

125 G/4 OZ BUTTER OR MARGARINE

275 ML/9 FL OZ MILK

265 G/8½ OZ SUGAR

500 G/1 LB MIXED DRIED FRUIT

1 TEASPOON MIXED SPICE

½ TEASPOON CINNAMON

65 ML/2½ FL OZ WHISKEY

1 SCANT TEASPOON BICARBONATE OF SODA

2 EGGS, BEATEN

265 G/8½ OZ SELF-RAISING FLOUR

265 G/8½ OZ PLAIN FLOUR

1 Place the butter or margarine, milk, sugar, fruit and spices in a saucepan, bring to the boil, cover and simmer for 5 minutes. Cool a little, then stir in the whiskey and bicarbonate of soda and allow to cool completely.

2 Add the beaten eggs and mix well. Sift the flours together and fold into the mixture, then spoon into a greased and bottom-lined 20 cm/8 inch cake tin.

3 Bake the cake in a preheated moderate oven at 180°C (350°F) Gas Mark 4 for 1 hour or until a skewer inserted in the centre comes out clean. Leave to cool in the tin.

Makes a 20 cm/8 inch cake

Whiskey Wafers

250 G/8 OZ CLEAR HONEY
250 G/8 OZ SUGAR
50 G/2 OZ BUTTER
300 G/10 OZ PLAIN FLOUR
1 TEASPOON BAKING POWDER
½ TEASPOON BICARBONATE OF SODA
2 TEASPOONS GROUND CINNAMON
½ TEASPOON GROUND CLOVES
½ TEASPOON GROUND CARDAMOM
125 ML/4 FL OZ WHISKEY
125 G/4 OZ BLANCHED ALMONDS, SLIVERED
150 G/5 OZ CHOPPED MIXED CANDIED PEEL

1 Place the honey, sugar and butter in a saucepan and heat gently until the butter melts, stirring constantly. Remove from the heat and cool to lukewarm.

2 Sift the flour with the baking powder, soda and spices, and stir in. Add the whiskey, almonds and peel and blend well. Chill for several hours.

3 Using 2 teaspoons dipped in hot water, spoon the mixture onto greased baking sheets and flatten slightly. Bake in a preheated moderately hot oven at 190°C (375°F) Gas Mark 5 for 10 minutes, or until lightly browned on top.

4 Cool for a minute before removing to wire racks. These are ideal served with ice cream.

Makes about 70

Irish Coffee Sorbet

An unusual but refreshing sorbet.

50 G/2 OZ MEDIUM-GROUND COFFEE
125 G/4 OZ SOFT BROWN SUGAR
2 TABLESPOONS WHISKEY
2 EGG WHITES

1 Place the medium-ground coffee into a saucepan and pour in
600 ml/1 pint water and bring to the boil. Remove the pan
from the heat and leave the coffee to infuse for 15 minutes.
2 Strain the coffee into a bowl. Stir in the sugar and the whiskey.
Put the bowl into the freezer until the sorbet has almost frozen.
3 Whisk the egg whites until stiff. Whisk the coffee mixture
and then fold in the whisked egg whites.
4 Pour the sorbet into a rigid freezer-proof container and return to
the freezer until solid. Store in the freezer until required.

Serves 4

Irish Coffee

An excellent after dinner drink.

SUGAR, TO TASTE
150 ML / ¼ PINT HOT STRONG, BLACK COFFEE
45 ML / 1½ FL OZ IRISH WHISKEY
1 TABLESPOON THICK DOUBLE OR WHIPPING CREAM

1 Warm a stemmed goblet glass and put in the sugar, to taste. Add the hot coffee to within 3 cm/1½ inches of the top, stir well to dissolve the sugar.

2 Add the Irish Whiskey to fill up to 1 cm/½ inch below the rim. Hold a teaspoon with its curved side uppermost across the top of the glass tilting a little downwards to the hot liquid. Dribble the cream over the teaspoon so that it settles in the top of the coffee but does not sink into it.

3 Do not stir, but drink the whiskey-coffee through the cream.

Serves 1

Peaches Steeped in Whiskey

*Vanilla sugar can be made by adding 1 to 2 vanilla
pods to a jar of sugar.*

250 G / 8 OZ VANILLA SUGAR
500 ML / 17 FL OZ IRISH WHISKEY
12 RIPE PEACHES
3 x 1 LITRE / 1¾ PINT AIRTIGHT KILNER JARS

1 Dissolve the sugar in 600 ml (1 pint) cold water over a low heat.
Bring to the boil and simmer for 1 minute. Crack the vanilla pod
open, but do not split them, add to the syrup, pour in
the whiskey and mix well.
2 Skin the peaches by putting them in boiling water for 1 minute, then
plunge into cold water and the skins should be removed easily.
3 Arrange the peaches in a jar and pour over the whiskey mixture.
Seal the jar and place in a cool, dark place for at least a
week before serving. Store for up to 1 month.
Serves 8

Tipsy Marmalade

1.5 KG/3 LB SEVILLE ORANGES
1 GRAPEFRUIT
8 TABLESPOONS LEMON JUICE
3.5 LITRES/6 PINTS WATER
2 KG/6 LB PRESERVING SUGAR
150 ML/¼ PINT WHISKEY

1 Squeeze the juice from the oranges and grapefruit and pour into a large preserving pan. Tie the pips in a piece of muslin and add to the juice in the pan. Add the lemon juice. Thinly slice the orange and grapefruit peel and add to the pan. Pour over the water, bring to the boil and simmer for 1½ hours until the peel has softened.

2 Remove the muslin bag of pips and squeeze the juice into the pan by pressing it between 2 wooden spoons. Add the sugar and heat gently, stirring until the sugar has dissolved. Pour in the whiskey.

3 Bring to the boil and boil rapidly for 20 minutes until setting point is reached, 104°C (220°F) on a sugar thermometer, or when a little is poured on to a cold saucer wrinkles when pushed with a finger. Remove the scum from the top of the marmalade. Allow to cool slightly and pour into hot sterilized jars.

4 Cover with waxed discs and cellophane secured with elastic bands and label. Tie ribbon around the neck of the jars.

Makes approximately 4½ kg/10 lb

Index

Weights and Measures

In this book, both metric and Imperial measures are used.
When working from the recipes, follow one set of measures only,
and not a mixture of both, as they are not interchangeable.

Notes for American and Australian Users

In America, the 8 fl oz measuring cup is used. In Australia, metric
measures are used in conjunction with the standard 250 ml measuring
cup. The Imperial pint, used in Britain and Australia, is 20 fl oz,
while the American pint is 16 fl oz.

The British standard tablespoon, which has been used throughout this
book, holds 17.7 ml, the American 14.2 ml, and the Australian 20 ml.
A teaspoon holds approximately 5 ml in all three countries

British	American	Australian
1 teaspoon	1 teaspoon	1 teaspoon
1 tablespoons	1 tablespoon	1 tablespoon
2 tablespoons	3 tablespoons	2 tablespoons
3½ tablespoons	4 tablespoons	3 tablespoons
4 tablespoons	5 tablespoons	3½ tablespoons

An Imperial/American Guide to Solid and Liquid Measures

Imperial	American	Imperial	American
Solid Measures		*Liquid Measures*	
1 lb butter	2 cups	¼ pint	⅔ cup
1 lb flour	4 cups	½ pint	1¼ cups
1 lb granulated		¾ pint	2 cups
sugar or caster		1 pint	2½ cups
sugar	2 cups	1½ pints	3¾ cups
1 lb icing sugar	3 cups	2 pints	5 cups
8 oz rice	1 cup		(2½ pints)